An Easy Guide To Programming in C

Second Edition

Written, designed, edited and illustrated by

Martin J. Gentile

Dedication

I would like to dedicate this book to the students of the Programming
Club at Haygrove School, Bridgwater, to whom I hope this book will serve as an introductory guide to the language of C.

Acknowledgments

I am heartily thankful to Ben Collinge and the ICT department at Haygrove School, whose encouragement and support enabled me to start the School's Programming Club in January 2012. After the first month, we had already learnt a good grounding in C.

I am very grateful to Jacob Hatzidogiannakis who introduced me to Objective-C and encouraged me to start running the Programming club, from which the idea for this book was borne.

Table of Contents

Preface to Second Edition

I have not introduced any major changes to the structure or content of this book, but I have clarified a few points in order to help the reader. I have detailed further how to install and use Code::Blocks, added a more exericses and programming ideas to the end of sections and added a few more explanatory notes.
I would like to thank everyone who drew my attention to errors or suggested improvements. These have all been implemented and will help improve the reading experience.

Martin J. Gentile
March 2012

Preface to First Edition

About This Book

This book assumes no prior knowledge of programming and introduces the reader to the computer language of C. By the end of this book, the reader should be acquainted with everything a programmer needs to know in order to produce simple programs in C. Reference is made to C's more complex aspects, but these are beyond the scope of this book. This book was written originally for a group of pupils, aged 11-15 years old for an after-school programming club but it is also relevant to undergraduate university students, or other adults who are completely new to the language of C. Within the programming club referred to in this introduction, some harboured ambitions to work for Apple; some were already developers for Google or Apple; and some just wanted or needed a leg-up in order to discover the joys of programming for themselves.

About the Author

Martin J. Gentile is a masters graduate in physics from Exeter University. For part of his degree, he studied at Iowa State University in Ames, Iowa, USA. His background is in theoretical physics and his particular strengths include pure and applied mathematics and programming. He knows many computer languages and has developed many programs over the years. His first program was written when he was eight years old, using an old Amstrad 386 computer to write in GW-BASIC! Currently, he writes programs in C, various types of Fortran, various types of BASIC, and is learning the Objective-C and Python languages.

How This Book is Organized

This book is organised into four distinct chapters:

Chapter 1 introduces programming in general, why we do it, what its purpose is, helpful techniques for approaching writing programs and the tools for writing programs in C.

Chapter 2 details the basics of the C programming language and contains a good grounding to produce programs.

Chapter 3 contains slightly more advanced topics in order to push this knowledge further, in order to build more efficient program.

Lastly, Chapter 4 introduces (but does not detail) some more advanced concepts of the C programming language for the reader's interest and to suggest further reading.

Exercises and Examples

Within every section of this book is at least one example of a real working program and an exercise for the reader to have an attempt at. These exercises are designed to strengthen the reader's programming skills, applying the knowledge learnt in the previous section, chapter or chapters. These increase in rigour throughout the book and some build upon each other. I encourage the reader therefore, to work his or her way through this book, attempting the exercises as they come up. The example programs are there for guidance and I would also encourage the reader therefore to copy and adapt these programs in order to attempt the exercises.

Font Conventions

For text directed to the reader as prose, this typeface is used.

```
For text directed to the reader as examples of programming in C, this typeface is used.
```

Comments and Questions

If there are any issues arising from this book, or if you have any comments or questions, please do not hesitate to e-mail me at the following address:

martin.gentile@alumni.exeter.ac.uk

Chapter 1

The Basics of Programming

1.1 How a Computer Works

Nowadays, computers are very complicated pieces of equipment and it seems hardly anybody gives a second thought to how they work; if they ever do, they might find the computer so baffling, that they are scared off again. However, the computers of today really do work on the same simple principals as each other. Every computer has:

- A central processing unit (CPU) which does all the work
- Read Only Memory (ROM) which has boot instructions
- Random Access Memory (RAM) which the computer runs programs from
- An Hard Disk Drive (HDD) for semi-permanent storage

1.2 How a Computer Language Works

Every computer language is designed for humans to be able to give the computer instructions. It is far easier to enter words than talking to the computer in its own language: binary! So we haven't got to talk to the computer in binary, CPUs have been developed, so that characters mean combinations of binary numbers. This is called machine code and can be read directly by the CPU. This is still difficult for humans to handle, so languages have been developed by assigning words and characters to mean combinations of machine code. C is just such a language and is illustrated in figure 1.1

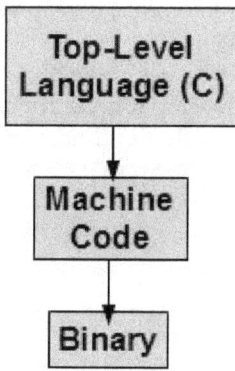

Figure 1.1: Where C fits in the computer's instruction hierarchy

1.3   Programming Approach

When writing programs, first identify your problem to solve. What do you want your program to do? Secondly, break your program idea down into small chunks. Draw out a flowchart. Will it work? What necessary steps have I got to involve? What areas of my program will require the hardest work? Are there any potential problems? Thirdly, write your main program and functions. Write in comments to help you along the way. Fourthly, test-run and debug your program. Are there any problems? Where are these problems, if any? Can I solve them? Lastly, once the program is finished, compile it into an executable file. Your program is now finished and ready to export to other computers!

1.4   Flowcharts

Flowcharts are useful for visualising how a program is going to work. There are several shapes for computer flowcharts; here are just a few:

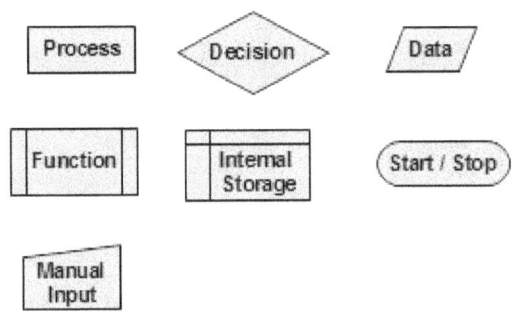

Figure 1.2: Six shapes used for drawing flowcharts. These are connected by arrows.

1.5   C Compilers

In order to write programs in C, you'll need a compiler to do it. To write and run programs, I recommend using Code::Blocks. It's free and available from www.codeblocks.org. It runs under Windows/Mac OS/Linux and you can adapt it for many different projects and languages, including OpenGL and Objective-C. If you're using Windows, open the website, then go to 'downloads', then 'binaries'. Make sure that you download and install the version with MinGW included. MinGW is actually a collection of compilers and it is Code::Blocks which runs this in order to make your programs. One can also download and install MinGW separately, from www.mingw.org. Once Code::Blocks is installed, create a new project. Click 'Console Application'. Select the 'C' language. Give the project a title and choose a sensible directory. Lastly, click 'Finish'. This will then create a very simple C program (called 'Hello World') to help you start writing your program. Look up the native documentation for further guidance with Code::Blocks.

If you're using a Mac and you want to go on to develop iPhone apps, then use XCode 4. This is also free and available at developer.apple.com/xcode. Another compiler out there is Microsoft Visual C++, but it doesn't work quite so well as Code::Blocks.

Chapter 2

Basic Programming in C

2.1 Basic Programming Layout in C

A C program is comprised of three main sections:

1. The pre-amble at the top of the program
2. The main program
3. Your own functions after the main loop

2.1.1 Pre-Amble

The pre-amble is itself comprised of four sections:

1. An introduction at the top of the program
2. Include statements for header files
3. Declarations of any special types to use in the program
4. Prototypes of functions to use later

Introduction

Here you introduce the program. /* */ or // means a comment. You can put whatever you want inside the two stars or after the double forward slashes and it won't be read by the computer. Comments are for your own benefit, so you can read the program more easily at a later date. Template for an introduction:

```
/*************************************************/
/* Title: [Your title here]                      */
/* Author: [Your name here]                      */
/* Date Written: [Date]                          */
/* Description: [Description of your program]     */
/*************************************************/
```

Include Statements

Here we bring in files (called header files, with extension .h) which contain all the commands we're going to use within our program. In C, always include the standard input/output and standard library header files like so:

```
#include <stdio.h>
#include <stdlib.h>
```

Any other header files should also be put here. A list of common ones to use include string.h, math.h, time.h and dos.h. These contain other commands which are used in this book.

Global Declarations and Definitions

Here we declare any structures or special types of things to use in the **entire** program. For example,

```
typedef enum{0 = 'true', 1 = 'false'}
```

would enable me to refer to the number 0 as 'true' and 1 as 'false' within the program itself, to make the programming easier.

Prototype functions

If we have defined our own functions to perform a specific task within the program, then we need to prototype (announce that we're going to use) them here. See Section 2.9 for more details.

2.1.2 Main Program

As the name suggests, this is the main part of the program. Here is a basic template:

```
int main(void){
    [your code here]
    return 0; //Quits the program
}
```

All of the main program is contained within these two curly braces. N.B. At the end of each line in C, always remember put a semi-colon (;)!

Declare Variables

At the very start of the main program, list all the variables you're going to use in the main program. Example:

```
int main(void){

    int age=13; //Creates an integer called 'age' and sets it to 13.
    float fraction=0.5; //Creates a float called 'fraction' and sets it to 0.5.
    char name[5]; //Create a string of character 5 letters long called 'name'.
    char initial = 'A' //Creates a character called 'initial' and sets it to A.
```

Example

Let's do an example of a simple program, the result of which is to put "Hello! I am 13 years old" on the screen.

```
#include <stdio.h>
#include <stdlib.h>

int main(void){                     //This starts the main program
    int age = 13; //Declare and initialise our integer number variable to 13.
    printf("Hello! I am %d years old.", age); //Put this message on screen
    return 0;                    // This quits the program
}
```

2.1.3   Functions

After the main program, we define our functions. See Section 2.9 for more details about making your own functions.

2.1.4   Good Programming Practise

There are three main top-tips to make your programs look neater and easier to read.

Indentation and Spacing

It is very important to indent your code. This is so that you can see the program easily as a collection of parts, rather than as a solid block. Look at the example above. Within the two curly braces, the program is indented. If I had a sub-section to my program, (e.g. a for loop) I would indent that part of my code further. Indentation doesn't actually *do*anything as such in C, but it is vital in other languages such as Python, so I also highly recommend doing so now to get into the habit of doing it.

Variable names

When declaring variables, call them sensible names, not arbitrary names. For example, `char hair_colour` is a much more descriptive and therefore sensible choice than `char a`. Conventially, when arbitrary number variables are declared for lots of different uses, integers are declared as i, j, k, etc. and floats are declared as a, b, c, etc.

Comments

One top tip: use comments as often as possible! These not only remind you at a later date what each line of code does, but tell other people what each line of code does too.

2.2   Variables, Inputs and Outputs

2.2.1   Variables

What is a variable?

A variable is essentially a number or a character which is given a particular value within the program. For example, if we had an integer variable x, we could give it the value '5' by writing x=5within the program. Or we could have a character which we could give the value 'm' by writing `test_character = 'm'`. The value of a variable is changeable, so we can re-assign the value of a variable at any time.

What types of variables are there?

There are essentially five types of variables in C. A summary of these variable types, declarers and identifiers is given in table 2.1 below:

Type	Declarer	Identifier
Integer	int	%d
Float	float	%f
Double	double	%lf
Character	char	%c
String	char	%s

Table 2.1: A summary of all variable types, declarers and identifiers

N.B. Strings are really an array of characters and need to be given a length. Example:

```
char name[5];
```

would declare a string (called 'name' five characters long).

What are declarers?   Each type of variable has to be declared before it can be used, using a declarer. After the declarer comes the name(s) of the variable(s). See table 2.1 for the different declarers.

What are identifiers?   Variables need to be handled in the right way within a program. To use variables, one must use an identifier. For example, in order to print our string `name` (section 2.1.2) we need to use the string identifier, %s:

```
printf("%s", name);
```

This would put whatever is contained within the string `name` on the screen. If we wanted to print our string `name` and our integer variable x together separated with a space, we would write:

```
printf("%s %d", name, x);
```

We can print as many variables as we want on the screen with a single `printf` statement.

2.2.2   Inputs

In order for the program to use any information, it must be given information to process first. The way it gets this information is from an input. Here I introduce a few useful functions to give information to the program.

scanf

scanf is a very basic function to scan in an input from the keyboard. How to use it:

```
scanf("%d %s", &integer, string);
```

Notice how our identifiers are used! Within the quotes indicates what we're looking for from the keyboard. In this case, we want to take in an integer, followed by a space, followed by a string. So within the quotes we have a %d for an integer, then a space, then a %s. These need to be called something, so we've called them 'integer' and 'string' respectively.

N.B. When **scanning in integers** , there is always & before the variable name!

fgets and sscanf

`fgets` takes in everything from the keyboard or elsewhere, regardless of what it looks like and stores it as a string. It is more powerful than `scanf` in that it can take in entire sentences rather than just words; but it can't scan for numbers. Therefore, we can use `sscanf` to analyse what `fgets` has taken in. Thus:

```
fgets(line, sizeof(line), stdin);
sscanf(line, "%d %s", &input_integer, input_string);
```

In this example, `fgets` has taken in everything from the keyboard (called `stdin`, meaning 'standard input') and stored it as a string called `line`. Then, `sscanf` looks at `line` and looks for an integer followed a string separated by a space. It then calls the integer `input_integer` and the string `input_string`.

2.2.3 Outputs

The most basic output function is `printf`. This function writes to the screen. Example:

```
printf("Hello World! My name is &s I am %d years old.", name, age);
```

would put, "Hello World! My name is Anna I am 12 years old." on the screen (provided that the string `name` contained the text, 'Anna' and the `age` integer was set equal to 12).

Exercises

1. Write a chat bot program, which asks for your name, age and date of birth in a conversational manner. Print this information to the screen. You will need to use `printf` and `scanf`, together with integer and string variables.
2. Adapt this program to include `fgets` and `sscanf` instead of `scanf`.
3. Trying getting the computer to ask you other questions such as favourite food, colour, etc. Store these answers and do something with them.

2.3   Maths in C

Simple maths is crucial within programming. Without it, very few programs can be analysed. Here is a brief introduction to maths in C.

2.3.1   Operators

Symbol	+	-	*	/	=	==	%
Meaning	Plus	Minus	Multiply	Divide	Become this	Equal to this?	Remainder

Table 2.2: All the mathematical operators needed for basic calculations.

Why have two equals signs?

= means "this is it; become this!" == means "is this the same as this?".
   Example: `if(y=3);` would set y equal to 3. `if(y==3);` would check to see whether y is already equal to 3 or not.

2.3.2   Types of numbers

In C, there are two types of numbers:

1. Integers (whole numbers, like 1, 2, 3, etc.)
2. Floating-points (like 1.0, 1.1, 1.2, 3.14159 etc.)

   Integers are declared like this:

```
int i, j, k; //This creates three integer variables called i, j and k.
```

   Floats are declared like this:

```
float x, y, z; //This creates three float variables called x, y and z.
```

   There is also a another type of number called a double, short for 'doubly-long floating point number'. They are sometimes used for extra accuracy in calculation, but are not used in this book. For reference, doubles are declared like this:

```
double u, v, w; //This creates three double variables called u, v and w.
```

   Doubles are also referred to as long floats within C itself, with the identifier `%lf` instead of `%f` for a float.

2.3.3   Maths and Variables

Assigning Values to Number Variables

To set a variable to a particular value, we use the = operator:

```
i = 4;
j = 2;
```

Sets the variables i and j to 1 and 2 respectively.

Adding and Subtracting Variables

Just like in usual maths, we use the addition and subtraction signs to add and subtract variables from each other:

```
k = i + j;
```

So $k = 4 + 2 = 6$ (if i is equal to 4 and j is equal to 2).

```
k = i-j;
```

So $k = 42 = 2$ (if i is equal to 4 and j is equal to 2).

Multiplication and Division of Variables

```
k = i * j;
```

So k = 4 * 2 = 8 (if i is equal to 4 and j is equal to 2).

```
k = i / j;
```

So k = 4 / 2 = 2 (if i is equal to 4 and j is equal to 2).

Adding Number Variables to Themselves

There are two ways of doing this:

```
i = i + j; /* one way */
i += j;   /*another way*/
```

So i = 4 + 2 = 6 in either example shown (if i is equal to 4 and j is equal to 2).

Finding the Remainder

For this, we use the % operator.

```
j = 7 % 2;
```

Would make j equal to 1, because 7 divided by 2 is 3 remainder 1.

Exercise

Write a program which scans for an integer from the keyboard, then prints to screen a multiplication table from 1 to 12. For example:

```
>Please enter a number: 2

1x2 = 2
2x2 = 4
3x2 = 6
4x2 = 8
.

.

.

12x2 = 24
```

2.4 Program Flow

So far, we've only created programs which flow from start to finish. What we now want are programs which can run themselves or sections of themselves over and over again. We do this by introducing a loop. There are various types of loops out there; here are a few.

2.4.1 While Loop

This kind of loop runs whilst the conditions set are still being fulfilled (or 'true' in programming speak). When conditions are not 'true', then they are 'false'. These we like to call 'Boolean values' . A while loop template is shown below:

```
while ([condition]){
   [Commands in here to perform while condition is fulfilled]
}
```

Let's take an example:

```
int i=0;

while (i<5){
    printf("I love programming!\n"); //Prints this message, then a newline (\n)
    i++; //increases the integer i by 1 each time.
}
```

This program simply prints "I love programming!" out onto screen five times on a new line.

2.4.2 Infinite Loop

This is sometimes useful.

```
while{1}{
    [Your code here to be performed ad infinitum]
}
```

This loop will now run forever. In order to make it stop, we need to add a `break` statement, to make the program break out of the loop. The `break` statement is usually accompanied by an `if` statement (see Section 3.4 more further details). Here's an example:

```
int i=0; //Declare an integer called i.

while{1}{
    printf("I love programming!\n"); //Print this message on screen
    i++;                             //Increase i by 1.
    if(i>5){                         //If i is greater than 5...
        break;                       //...then exit the loop.
    }
}
```

This accomplishes the same task as the example in Section 2.4.1.

2.4.3 For loop

This is a slightly different kind of loop. It defines conditions at the start and runs a set number of times. In this example adapted from Section 2.4.1 again, the integer variable i starts at 0 (set by `i=0`) then increases in size by 1 (set by `++i`) every time the loop runs until it reaches 5, as set by `i<5`. Therefore, the loop is run 5 times:

```
for (i=0 ; i<5 ; ++i){ //Begin the loop and set the conditions.
    printf("I love programming!\n"); //Print this message on screen.
}
```

2.4.4 The goto Statement

The `goto` statement makes the program jump from one part of the program to another. It is entirely unnecessary to use goto statements in C and much easier to use while and for loops instead. They make the program difficult to follow and formatting is a nightmare. However, there are circumstances where it is simply easier to use a `goto` statement. When you must use one, here's how to use it properly:

First, identify where you want the program to jump to. Second, add a label like so:

```
example_label:
```

Third, put a `goto` statement in the desired place in the program, followed by the label, like so:

```
goto example_label;
```

Adapting our example from the Section 2.4.1 again:

```
int i=0;

label_one:
printf("I love programming!\n");
i++; //Increase i by 1.

if(i<5){
    goto label_one;
}
```

Again, this program prints out the message five times on screen.

Exercises

1. Write a program which asks the user a question, then prints his or her answer on screen 10 times and ten times only. Do you prefer using a `while` loop, infinite `while` loop, `for` loop, or the `goto` statement? Can you make all of them work? Which requires the least typing?
2. Adapt your multiplication table program from the last exercise to encorporate a loop in order to print the table. How many lines of code have you saved?
3. Make a count-down program which counts down from a user-specified number to zero before making a rocket blast off! A simple graphic for a rocket can be a T with exclamation marks underneath it.

2.5   More on Characters & Strings

2.5.1   Words and Letters

Single Characters

Declared by `char`, identifier %c. Example:

```
char initial; // Declares a single-character variable called "initial"
```

Strings of Characters

Declared by `char`, identifier %s. Example:

```
char name[10]; // Declares a string variable called 'name'
```

This new variable called `name` and is 10 characters long, as indicated in the square brackets.

Name Program

```
#include <stdio.h>
#include <stdlib.h>

int main(void){

    char initial;  // Defines a character called initial.
    char name[10]; // Defines a string called name.

    printf("What is your name? Please enter your initial, followed by your surname:\n");

    scanf("%c %s", &initial, name); // Reads in information from keyboard.
    // Puts your initial + name on screen.
    printf("Hello %c %s! I am a computer.\n", initial, name);

    return 0; // Quits the program
}
```

Example output:

```
What is your name?
>M Gentile
Hello M Gentile! I am a computer.
```

Exercise

Write a program containing an already-existing funny story to print out, with some (say, 10) adjectives missing. Ask the user to enter the missing adjectives. Next, use these adjectives to fill the holes and then print the resulting funny story!

2.6 Example Programs for I/O & Maths

In order to make things make a little more sense, here are a few examples of simple programs using everything we've used so far.

2.6.1 Poetry Program

Functions used: `printf`, `scanf` for strings (%s).

```
/****************************************************************/
/*Title: Poetry Program                                        */
/*Author: Mr. M Gentile                                        */
/*Date: 30-1-12                                                */
/*Description: This is a program used to write poems           */
/****************************************************************/


int main(void){ //Begin main program

    char name[20], word1[20]; //declares two strings, 20 letters long.

    printf("What is your name?\n"); //printf means "put this on screen"!
    scanf("%s", name); //Takes in your name
    printf("Hello %s! Type in a word that rhymes with 'me':", name);
    scanf("%s", word1); //Takes in your word
    printf("A poem by %s.\n", name);
    printf("Programming used to frighten me,\n"); //Puts the poem on screen
    printf("But now I'm happy as a %s", word1);

    return 0; //Quits the program
} //End of main program
```

Exercise

Can you improve upon this program? Try adding verses.

2.6.2 Multiplier program

Functions used: `printf` and `scanf` for integers (%d).

```
/********************************************************************/
/*Program Name: Multiplier                                         */
/*Author: M. Gentile                                               */
/*Date: 30-01-2012                                                 */
/*Description: This program allows the user to multiply two numbers together.*/
/********************************************************************/

#include <stdio.h>
#include <stdlib.h>


int main(void){ //Begin main program

    int input1=0, input2=0; //Define two number variables

    printf("Please enter two numbers: "); //Put this on screen
```

```
    scanf("%d %d", &input1, &input2); //Scan for two numbers from keyboard
    printf("%dx%d=%d\n", input1, input2, input1*input2); //Print the result

    return 0; //Quit
} //End of main program
```

Exercises

1. As well as multiplication (*) as in this example, try turning this program into a basic calculator, handing addition (+) subtraction (-) and division (/) and giving the user the choice.
2. Write a program to estimate the height of an object with a given angle and distance, using $Opposite = tan(angle) \times Adjacent$. The three trigonometric functions in C are entered as sin(), cos() and tan() with the angle inside the round brackets.

2.6.3   Space Commando Program

This is a two-player game, where one player is the space commando trying to find the alien and the other is the alien trying to evade capture. Firstly, the alien player enters their co-ordinates in space e.g. 2 4. Next, the screen is cleared. Then, the space commando player enters their co-ordinates e.g. 2 6. The distance between the two players is calculated by pythagoras (in our case, 2 units). If it is less than a certain 1.5 units, then the space commando has found the alien and the game ends. If not, then the game continues. After the alien is found, the two players swap around.

Functions used: printf, scanf, for loops, while loops and simple maths.

```
/***********************************************************/
/*Title: Space Commando                                    */
/*Author: Mr. M. Gentile                                   */
/*Date: 30-1-12                                            */
/*Description: This program allows players to search for*/
/*     aliens in the midst of space!                       */
/***********************************************************/

#include <stdio.h>
#include <stdlib.h>

int main(void){ //Start main program

    int i; //define an integer called 'i'
    int alien_x, alien_y; //co-ords for alien
    int commando_x, commando_y; //co-ords for commando
    float distance; //distance between two N.B. a float number

    while(1){ //Loop indefinitely

        printf("Alien player! Enter your two co-ordinates separated with a space: ");
        scanf("%d %d", &alien_x, &alien_y); //Take in alien's co-ords
        for(i=0;i<100;i++){ //Clear the screen, so the commando player
            printf("\n");   //can't see the co-ords of the alien.
        }

        printf("Commando player! Enter your two co-ordinates separated with a space: ");
        scanf("%d %d", &commando_x, &commando_y); //Take in commando's co-ords
        for(i=0;i<100;i++){ //Clear the screen, so the alien player
            printf("\n");   //can't see the co-ords of the commando.
        }
```

```
    /*Compute the distance in-between the alien and the commando using Pythagoras*/
    distance=sqrt((commando_x-alien_x)*(commando_x-alien_x)+
                  (commando_y-alien_y)*(commando_y-alien_y));

    //Show the distance between each
    printf("Your are now %f space units apart.\n", distance);

    if(distance<1.5){ //If this distance is less than 1.5 units, then...
        printf("Alien found!"); //show this message and...
        return 0; //Quit the program
    }
    else{ //If the distance isn't less than 1.5, then go again.
        printf("What are your new co-ordinates?\n");
    }
}

return 0;
}
```

Exercises

1. Can you try turning this program into a 3D program, instead of 2D?
2. Can you add more players to make it two aliens vs. two commandos?
3. Can you make it the best of three games?
4. Can you find a better way to clear the screen than using the for loop?

   Hint: For exercise 4, you will need to include the <dos.h> header file, then use the cls (clear screen) function like so:

```
system("cls");
```

2.7   Comparing and Handling Strings

2.7.1   The Header File

For all the functions in this chapter, you will need to add at the top of the program:

```
#include <string.h>
```

This header file includes all the functions you need to handle strings (words).

2.7.2   strcpy

Used for copying one string into another. Example:

```
strcpy(string_to_be_written_to, "[whatever you want to say here]");
```

2.7.3   strcat

Adds one string onto the end of the other. Example:

```
strcat(string_to_be_added_to, "[whatever you want]");
```

2.7.4   strcmp

Compares one string against another, to see whether they are equal N.B. Strings are case sensitive!

```
strcmp(string_to_be_compared, "rainy")
```

This function returns (becomes equal to) a '0' (true) if they are equal and a '1' (false) otherwise. These values can be set to be something more manageable using enum:

2.7.5   enum

The enum function allows you to set a number equal to a magic word. Example:

```
typedef enum {true=0, false=1} true_false;
```

would mean that within the compiler from now on the computer will recognise 'true' and 'false' being equal to '0' and '1' respectively.

2.8   Example Programs Using String Functions

2.8.1   Weather Program

Functions used: `strcmp`, `printf`, `scanf`.

```
/*****************************************************/
/*Title: Weather program*/
/*Author: Mr. M. Gentile*/
/*Date: 30-01-12*/
/*Description: This program asks what the weather's like*/
/*****************************************************/

#include <stdio.h>
#include <stdlib.h>
#include <string.h> // N.B. We need this in order to use the strcmp function.

typedef enum{true=0,false=1} true_false; //This defines our Boolean values

int main(void){

    char weather[50]; //Input variable (a string)

    printf("How's the weather outside?\n"); //Asks the question
    scanf("%s", weather); //Scans for input from keyboard
    if(strcmp(weather, "raining")==true){ //If user entered "rainy" then...
        printf("Stay inside!"); //print a statement.
    }
    if(strcmp(weather, "sunny")==true){ //If user entered "sunny" then...
        printf("Go outside and enjoy it!"); //print a statement.
    }
    return 0; //Quit.
}
```

Exercise

Can you add more weather types to this program and make it non-case sensitive?

2.8.2   Artificial Intelligence

Functions used: `printf`, `scanf`, `strcpy`, `strcat`.

```
/*****************************************************/
/*Title: Artificial Intelligence                    */
/*Author: Mr. M. Gentile                            */
/*Date: 17-02-12                                    */
/*Description: This programs uses fgets to          */
/*             take an input from the keyboard       */
/* instead of scanf. fgets is a much better function!*/
/*****************************************************/

#include <stdio.h>
#include <stdlib.h>
#include <string.h>

int main(void){
```

```c
    int i;
    char chat1[200], chat2[200], chat3[300];
    char data1[50], data2[50], data3[50], data4[50], data5[50];

    strcpy(data1,"Why");
    strcpy(data2,"Why is that");
    strcpy(data3,"Can you explain");
    strcpy(data4,"Can you say why");
    strcpy(data5,"What was the reason");

    printf("I would like to talk to you...\n");
    printf("Tell me anything silly that happened to you this week.\n");
    scanf("%s",chat1);

        printf("%s? ",data1);
        fgets(chat2, sizeof(chat2),stdin);
        strcat(chat3, chat2);

        printf("%s? ",data2);
        fgets(chat2, sizeof(chat2),stdin);
        strcat(chat3, chat2);

        printf("%s? ",data3);
        fgets(chat2, sizeof(chat2),stdin);
        strcat(chat3, chat2);

        printf("%s? ",data4);
        fgets(chat2, sizeof(chat2),stdin);
        strcat(chat3, chat2);

        printf("%s? ",data5);
        fgets(chat2, sizeof(chat2),stdin);
        strcat(chat3, chat2);

    printf("So, you told me ");
    printf("%s ",chat1);
    printf("The reason why was really given by your answer ");
    printf("%s ",chat3);
    printf("So there you go!\n");
    printf("Knowledge is power.");

    return 0;
}
```

Exercise

Can you make this program a bit more intelligent? Can you save parts of the conversation to file and then when it re-runs it checks to see whether you've entered what you're entering before? See Section 2.10 for saving to and loading from file!

2.9   Making Your Own Functions

2.9.1   What is a Function?

A function is simply a mini-program which returns a number to the main program. They are useful, because they help break the program down into manageable-sized chunks. For example, making a hot drink:

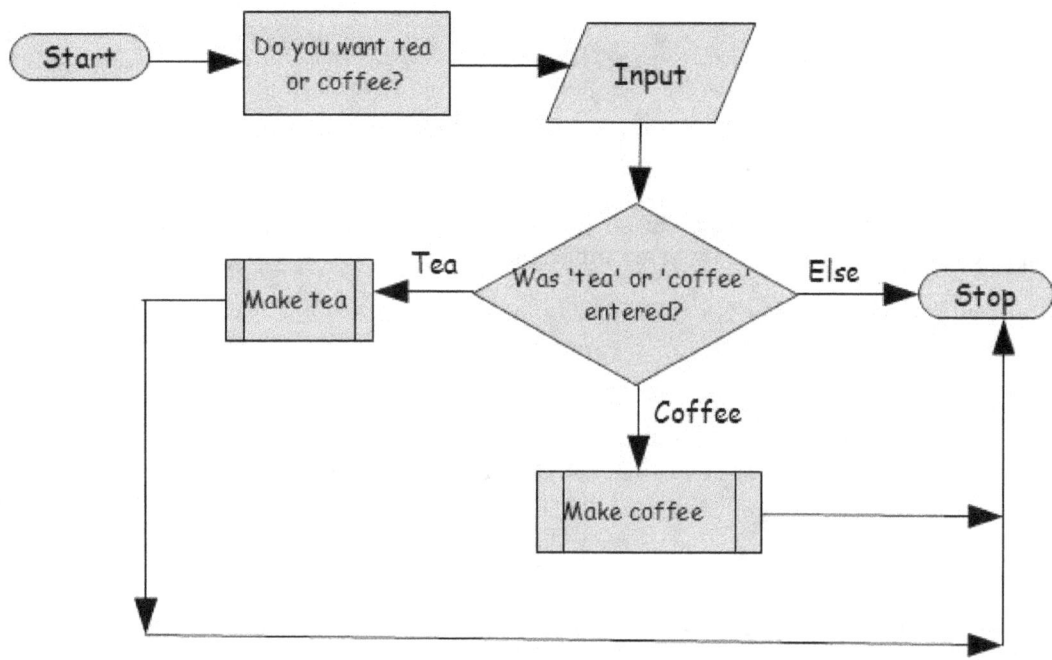

Figure 2.1: How functions break down a big task into manageable steps. The 'make tea' and 'make coffee' boxes are functions.

   Functions contain lots of standard instructions all linked in together to do just one task. This is very useful if we are going to want to do the same task more than once within the program: it saves a lot of typing!

2.9.2   Writing Functions in C

Prototyping

Functions usually return integer numbers. If they do, we declare our functions with the int declarer. But firstly, we need to prototype our functions, just before the int main(void) bit of the main program. We need to give the function a name. We also need to say what the function needs in order to do its job. This information is contained within the brackets. Example:

```
int example_one(int a, int b);
```

   This function is now called `example_one` and will take in two integers referred to as a and b within the function. N.B. It doesn't matter what you call these integers in the main program and you can give this function **any** two integers, no matter what they're called.

Making the Function

Now you need to put the function at the end of the main program, after the }. For example:

```
int example_one(int a, int b){
    [your code here]
    return [whatever value you want to return]
}
```

Calling Functions

Calling (using) functions within the main program is easy: just type the name of the function, then put inside the round brackets whatever you want to give it! For example:

```
int main(void){
    example_one(1,2);
    return 0;
}
```

This program will call (run) function `example_one`, feeding it the numbers 1 and 2 before quitting the program.

2.9.3   Example Program for a Function

In the following example, I have added a function to our multiplier program (see above). I have called it `multiply`. It takes in two integers and returns their product to the main program.

```
/*****************************************************************/
/*Program Name: Multiplier */
/*Author: M. Gentile */
/*Date: 30-01-2012 */
/*Description: This program allows the user to multiply two numbers together.*/
/*****************************************************************/

#include <stdio.h>
#include <stdlib.h>

int multiply(int a, int b); //Prototype our function

int main(void){ //Begin main program

    int input1=0, input2=0; //Define two number variables
    int result;

    printf("Please enter two numbers: "); //Put this on screen
    scanf("%d %d", &input1, &input2); //Scan for two numbers from keyboard
    result=multiply(input1,input2); //Call the function using the inputs
    printf("%dx%d=%d\n", input1, input2, result); //Print the result

    return 0; //Quit
}

//Our multiply function is below:
int multiply(int a, int b){
    int c=0;  //Declare an integer for the result
    c=a*b;    //Compute the result
    return c; //Result the result to the main program
}
```

Exercise

Take a look back over your artificial intelligence program. Can you put the `printf` `fgets` `strcat` blocks into a single function? This would save a lot of programming space for sure!

2.10 Saving to and Loading From File

Before we begin saving and loading files in C, I need to point out where the files will be saved and loaded from and to: all files should be in the "bin" then "debug" folder in the same as the directory as where your project is saved.

2.10.1 Declaring a File

First, we need to declare our file. This is just like declaring any other variable, such as `int`, `float` or even `char`. For files, we use the `FILE` declarer. For example:

```
FILE *InFile;
```

Will create a pointer (see Section 3.8) to a file we're going to call `InFile` in our program. It is **important** to declare the file pointer with a `*` before its name, but we can call the file whatever we want; again, see Section 3.8 for more details on pointers.

2.10.2 Saving to file

This is actual quite simple, but there is a little bit of jargon to cover. The main steps in saving are:

1. Open the file
2. Write to the file
3. Close the file

Opening the file is essential, closing the file is necessary. Without closing the file, you use up computer memory (RAM) and the whole system slows down. Eventually, it will crash! (I've seen this happen).

Opening

To open the file, we use the `fopen` function. We then assign our pointer `InFile` (see above) to the actual file. For example:

```
InFile = fopen("test_file.txt","w");
```

This opens (or creates if it doesn't exist) the file in the `w` or 'writing' mode. This mode wipes the file before writing to it. If this is not desired, there is another way of opening a file without clearing it: `a` or 'append' mode.

Writing

To write to the file, we use the `fprintf` function instead of `printf`. For example:

```
fprintf(InFile, "test 1,2,3 %d %s", an_int_variable, a_string_variable);
```

will print what we have in quotes to the file `InFile`.

Closing

Use the `fclose` function. Our `InFile` pointer is now pointing at our file. So all we do now is just use the `fclose` function on the pointer to our file. For example:

```
fclose(InFile);
```

It's as easy as that!

Example for Saving to File

```c
/*********************************************/
/* Title: Name-saver                         */
/* Author: M. Gentile                        */
/* Date: 26-2-12                             */
/* Description: This program save your name*/
/*    to file, then prints an evil message.*/
/*********************************************/

#include <stdio.h>
#include <stdlib.h>

int main(void){

    char name[30];
    FILE *OutFile; //Define our pointer to our file, calling it "OutFile"

    printf("What is your name?");
    scanf("%s", name);

    OutFile = fopen("name.txt","w"); //Opening input file in write mode

    fprintf(OutFile, "%s", name); //!!CRUCIAL PART!! Saves name to file.

    fclose(OutFile); //Closes the file

    //When complete, print this message
    printf("%s, I have remembered your name forever! Mwahuahuahua!\n", name);
    printf("(That is, until you run me again, by which time I'll have forgotten).");

    return 0;
}
```

Exercises

You have a choice! Either:

1. Write a program which allows the user to save their name, age, date of birth and postcode to file. Think carefully about the variable types involved.
2. Write a program which allows the user to save their conversations with the chat bot program created in Section 2.2.3.

In either case, remember where the file is stored (see the note at the top of Section 2.10). Adapt the above example if you find it helpful and remember to open the file after the program has run to check that it works.

2.10.3 Loading from file

Similarly, the main steps in loading from a file are:

1. Open the file
2. Read the file
3. Close the file

Opening

To open the file to load from it, we need to open in 'read' or r mode. For example:

```c
InFile = fopen("test_file.txt","r");
```

Reading

Here, we use the `fgets` and `sscanf` functions in order to read the file. For example:

```
fgets(line, sizeof(line), InFile); //Read one line of the file
sscanf(line, "%d %s", &integer1, string1); //Scans an integer, then a string
```

Closing

The same as saving:

```
fclose(InFile);
```

Example For Loading From File

```
/********************************************************************/
/* Title: Football Scores                                           */
/* Author: Mr. M. Gentile                                           */
/* Date: 26-2-12                                                    */
/* Description: This program loads one team name and score in the league table */
/* from a file.                                                     */
/********************************************************************/

#include <stdio.h>
#include <stdlib.h>

int main(void){

    int i, points; //Creates two integers
    char line[30], team[25]; //Creates two strings
    FILE *Scores //Declaring the file pointer

    //Opening the file
    Scores = fopen("football_scores.txt","r");

    //Reading the file
    fgets(line, sizeof(line), Scores); //Scans 1st line of file storing it in 'line'.
    sscanf(line, "%s %d", team, &points); //Scans team name and points from 'line'.

    //Closing the file again
    fclose(Scores);
}
```

Exercise

Add to your program created for Section 2.10.2 a function which loads the saved information from file again. You will need to use `fgets` and `sscanf` for this. Think carefully about the variable types involved.

2.10.4   A Better Way of Opening and Closing Files

It's much better to turn the loading or saving process into a function, so that the program can perform this task at any time. Also, it's a lot better to check to see whether the file was actually opened before proceeding. If there's an error, the program will crash and return 1. Another improvement is to open the file in a, or 'append' mode. That way, the file will not be wiped before you write to it. Sometimes you want it to be cleared, but other times you do not. In the whole-program example below, the program asks the user for his or her name and then saves their name to file permanently:

```c
/********************************************************/
/* Title: Name-saver 2                                  */
/* Author: M. Gentile                                   */
/* Date: 26-2-12                                        */
/* Description: This program save your name permanently */
/*    to file, then prints an evil message.             */
/********************************************************/

#include <stdio.h>
#include <stdlib.h>

int save(char a[30]); //Function prototype

int main(void){

    char name[30];

    printf("What is your name?");
    scanf("%s", name);
    save(name);

    //When name is saved, print this message
    printf("%s, I have remembered your name forever!\n");
    printf("Mwuhuahuahua!!");

    return 0;
}

int save(char to_save[30]){

    FILE *OutFile; //Define our pointer to our file, calling it "OutFile"

    printf("Saving your name to file..."); //Message on screen

    OutFile = fopen("name.txt","a"); //Opening input file in append mode.
    if(OutFile == NULL){ //If it doesn't open...
        printf("Could not open the input file"); //Error message if not opened
        return 1; //Exit, returning 1 instead of 0 to show error.
    }

    fprintf(OutFile, "%s", to_save); //!!CRUCIAL PART!! Saves name to file.

    fclose(OutFile); //Closes the file.

    return 0; //Stop the function and return to the main program.
}
```

Exercise

Modify your program from the previous exercise to incorporate this modular saving and loading process. How many lines of code have you saved?

2.11 Random Numbers

The function to produce numbers in C is called `rand()`. It works by consulting a random-number table stored within the computer, to produce an apparently random number. It works like this:

```
int random; //Declare an integer

random = rand()%100+1; //Set our integer equal to a random number, from 1-100.
```

The `100` after the `rand()` means, "Find me a random number up to (but not including) 100". The thing is, this also includes 0, so I'm really finding a random number between 0-99. Therefore, I've added a `1` after the `rand()%100`, in order to find a number between 1-100. There is another downside to using `rand()`: the computer uses the same random number the next time the program is run! To get around this, we start the computer looking at its random number table in a different place to usual. We do this by including the `<time.h>` header file and then seed the `rand()` function with a value of the computer's own time. Therefore, the random numbers will change every time the program is run. Because we've got to add extra lines in order to do this, we're going to put all this inner-workings into a separate function within the program to make things neater. Here's how we do it:

```
/* * * * * * * * * * * * * * * * * * * * * * * * * * * * * * * * * * * * *
* Title: Random Numbers
* Author: M. Gentile
* Date: 29th February 2012
* Description: This program generates a random number by calling a function.
* * * * * * * * * * * * * * * * * * * * * * * * * * * * * * * * * * * * * */

#include <stdio.h>
#include <stdlib.h>
#include <time.h>

int random(int a); //Prototype our random function for later

int main(void){ //Begin main program

    int test; //Declare an integer

//Call our function, assigning our integer to the value it returns:
    test = random(100); //In this case, ask for a number from 1-100

    printf("Your random number is: %d", test); //Print the number.

    return 0; //Quit.
}

int random(int a){ //Begin our random function.

//Seed rand() with time, so numbers are more random
    unsigned int iseed = (unsigned int)time(NULL);
    srand (iseed+1);

    return rand()%a+1; //Returns random number generated by rand() to main program
}
```

Exercise

Try turning this program into a lottery numbers generator, choosing 6 random numbers between 1 and 49.

2.12   Challenges!

Using your own creativity, write a program of your choice which uses as many of the functions as possible as outlined in this chapter. Here are some programming project ideas:

- Make a fully-functioning calculator, with memory which can be saved to and loaded from file.

- Write a program to find a user-specified number of prime numbers. For example, when the user enters '10', the first 10 prime numbers are displayed. Hint: You will need to use the % operator to determine that a certain number has got no remainder zeros when divided by .

- Improve on the Space Commando and Alien game, where you can save the game, load the scores and the player names.

- Make an encryption program, which encodes a secret message as put in by you and can decode it too.

- A quiz game, where the computer knows the answers and can give you a score as a percentage, with an appropriate message. As an extension, make the computer load the answers a text file. As a further extension, let the computer save new correct answers to file for future reference.

- A simple card game, such as blackjack (otherwise known as pontoon, or 21).

- Two player noughts and crosses, with dots, O's and X's being printed on the screen for the score.

- Two player connect four, with dots O's and X's printed on the screen for the score.

- Guess a number game, with the computer generating a random number for the player to guess.

- An artificial intelligence program with memory, so that it remembers past names of users and their past conversations.

For more advanced C functions and programming techniques which might be useful for these challenges, please see the following chapter.

2.12.1   Calculator Program Tips

The final input and output should look something like this:

```
Enter calculation (or press q to quit):
>5x7
5x7=35
Enter calculation (or press q to quit):
>107-52
107-52=55
Enter calculation (or press q to quit):
q

Process returned 0
```

As a tip, use int to declare the variables to start with, then expand to using strings later. Use this format to read in from the keyboard: %d%c%d for int, char, int to handle (for example) 5x5, 9/2 or even 6+7.

Chapter 3

Intermediate Programming in C

So far, we've looked at the very basics which C has to offer. But for more fluid and easy-to-write programs, we're going to need some of the things laid out in this chapter. Arrays are particularly useful and they explained in section 3.6.

3.1 Debugging Your Program

We've all had our own programs crash from time-to-time. When this happens, it's usually because of mistakes in the program itself, called bugs.

3.1.1 Finding Bugs

Before we can solve bugs in the program, we first need to find them. In order to find bugs, here's top tip: insert `return` functions into the program at various points to check just where the program stops working. Conventionally, when a program returns 0, it means that the program was completed successfully. With this in mind, insert returns of values other than zero. Try putting `return 1`, or `return 2` for example just before various suspect crash points. Then, when the program exits, with a "status 1" for example, you know that the program got to the point at which you inserted the code `return 1`. Then you move the return forward a line or two, until the program crashes again. By this process, you can find the line at which the program crashes. If the program still crashes, move the return function back a line, until the program exits with the value you want. Again, this is the 'Aha!' moment, when you have identified the problem line. The next step is simply to sort out the problem in the line.

3.1.2 Correcting Bugs in C

There are several common bugs in C; here are a few solutions to the most common problems:

Semi-Colons

One common error is caused by not ending the line with a semi-colon (;). Example:

```
printf("I love computers!")
```

The solution to this is simple: put a semi-colon (;) at the end of the line, in this case, just after the `printf` statement.

Mis-Spellings

Always check that the variable names used are the same as they were declared. Example:

```
int my_age=13;

printf("I am %d years old.", my_ahe);
```

Here we've accidentally typed in `my_ahe` instead of `my_age`. This also applies to functions. A typical example error is shown below:

```
fro(i=0; i<5 ; i++){
```

The word `for` is mis-spelt here. Make sure that functions are all spelt correctly.

Variables not declared

Make it your habit, whenever a new variable is used, to declare it at the top of the function or main program immediately. That way, you will never be using variables which are not yet declared.

& Trouble

Scanning in an integer, float, double or character (strings **exempt**) without a & preceding the variable name will result in an error. For example:

```
scanf("%d %c %s %f", int_one, char_one, string_one, float_one);
```

instead of

```
scanf("%d %c %s %f", &int_one, &char_one, string_one, &float_one);
```

Remember that strings don't need this, but every other variable type does.

Using the wrong type of equals sign

All too easy to do: there are two types in in C. For example, `int i==1;` would not set `i` equal to 1, but `int i=1;` would. Another example:

```
if(i=5){
    [Commands to do if i equals 5]
}
```

would not check to see whether `i` is **already** equal to 5, but would **set** `i` equal to 5. Therefore, this example `if` statement would be useless. Instead, we should have:

```
if(i==5){
    [Commands to do if i equals 5]
}
```

Missing quotes and brackets

All too often, quotes are started and then never stopped. Remember that all quotes and brackets come in pairs. These following lines will not work:

```
printf("I love computing!";
printf("I love computing!);
char test_char = '0;
if(test_char==28){
```

The first line will not work because of a missing). The second line will not work because of a missing ". The third line will not work because of a missing ' after the 0. The fourth line will work, but it won't ever exit the if statement, because of a missing }. Code::Blocks is very helpful in solving these problems, because whenever you open a bracket or a quote, it adds the closing bracket or quote automatically.

Exercise

Try debugging the following program to get it working on your computer. The code has seven bugs in it. Can you find the bugs? Can you correct the program so that it will work?

```
/* * * * * * * * * * * * * * * * * * * * * * * * * * * * * *
 * Title: Limerick
 * Author: M. Gentile
 * Date: 1st March 2012
 * Description: This program generates a Limerick if the user wants.
 * * * * * * * * * * * * * * * * * * * * * * * * * * * * * */

#include <stdio.h>
#include <stdlib.h>

int main(void){

    int choose;

    printf("Press 1 if you want me to give you a Limerick.);

    scanf("%d", choice);
    if(choice = 1){
        printf("There once was a lady called Bright\n")
        printf("Who could travel much faster than light.\n";
        printf("She started one day in the relative way,\n");
        printt("And arrived on the previous night.");
    }

    return 0;
}
```

3.2 ASCII

3.2.1 What is ASCII?

ASCII stands for "American Stand Code for Information Interchange". Essentially, every character we put on the screen from A to Z, is an ASCII character. There are even special characters out there, such as hearts (ASCII code 3), smiley faces (ASCII codes 1 and 2), even a degree sign (ASCII code 248). "Why are they assigned these numbers?" I hear you cry. Well, computers are all based on numbers. Single digit numbers, i.e. from 0-15. Yes, that's right, 15! "But 15's a 2-digit number!" I hear you say. Well, not for a computer. See, 15 is really 2x2x2x2-1 and is assigned the letter F. This is the hexadecimal system which computers count in: not from 0-9 like us, but from 0-F. Now, this base-16 system which the computers count in enables us to have 16 times 16 characters in our vocabulary: that is, 256 characters! 52 (uppercase and lowercase) are reserved for A-Z and 10 are for the numbers 0-9. Here's a figure showing what I mean:

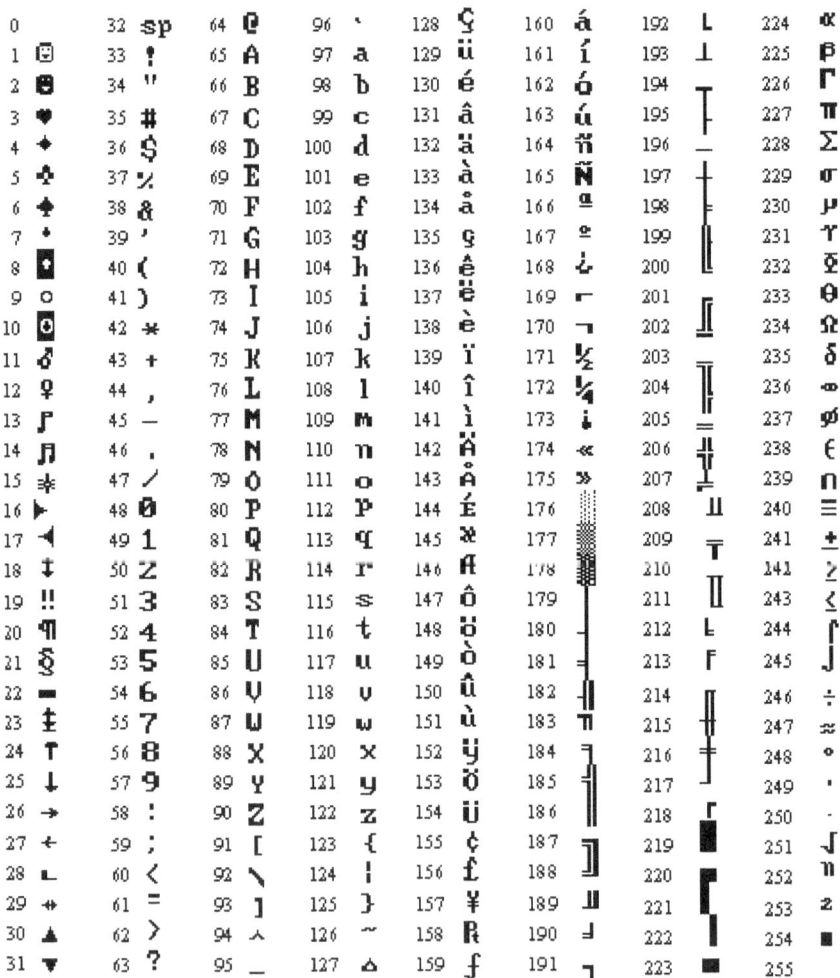

Figure 3.1: This figure shows all 256 ASCII characters, together with their respective codes.

3.2.2 Character to Integer Conversion

Look at the number '0' in the ASCII table. It has ASCII value 48. Believe it or not, these values are actually the **values** of these characters in programs. Therefore, we can change characters to numbers fairly easily, just by subtracting 48. For example:

```
char test; //Declare a character
int converted;
```

```
test = '5'; //Give our test character the character '5'

converted = test - 48;

printf("The value of '5' is %d", converted);
```

3.2.3 Simple Graphics

We can also use ASCII characters to create very simple graphics. In fact, characters 176-223 were designed specifically for this purpose in the early days of computing. Placed next to each other, ASCII characters can form some quite remarkable images. For example:

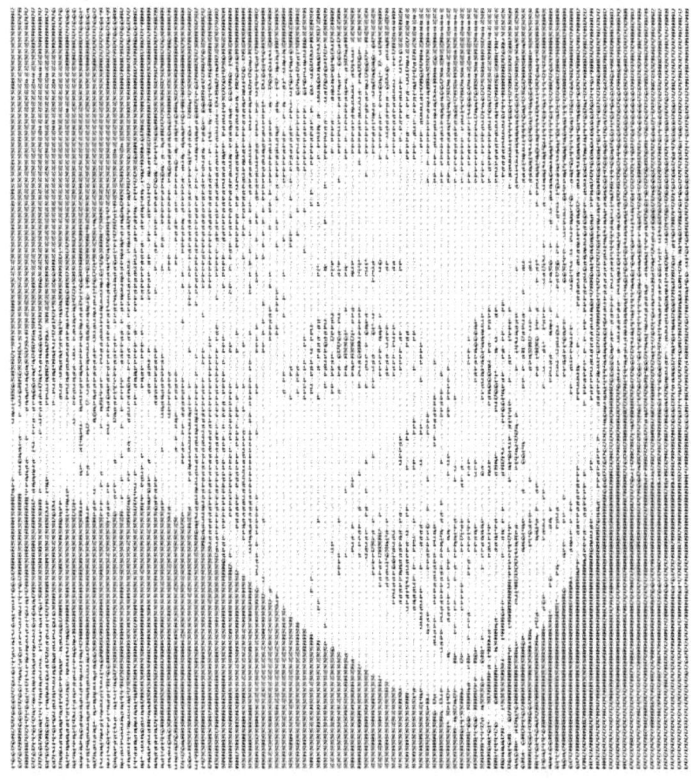

Figure 3.2: A picture of Albert Einstein, made from lots of ASCII characters with thanks to: www.degraeve.com.

Exercises

1. Random ASCII characters can be generated by printing characters with random integer values between 0 and 255, e.g. `printf("%c", rand()%256);`. Write a program which generates output that looks like the console output from the film The Matrix!
2. Using the ASCII table above (figure 3.1), write a program which will print out a rectangle, a square and a triangle one after another. What other shapes can you make?

3.3 #define Statement

This statement is placed at the very start of the program, before the main program. It is used for referring to a number which WON'T CHANGE during the course of the program. For example, π. C doesn't know what the value of π is offhand, so we need to tell it; with a define statement:

```
#define PI 3.14159265
```

Then, whenever we refer to PI during the rest of the program, the computer will know that PI means the same thing as 3.14159265. Notice that we've defined π in upper case; this is important.

We can also define macros, which act sort of like functions in the program. Here's an example to convert temperature, in degrees Fahrenheit to Celsius:

```
#define FTOC(x) (((x) - 32) * 0.55555555)
```

Then, in the main program, all we do to convert 50 degrees Fahrenheit to degrees Celsius is put FTOC(50), which of course would give us 10 degrees Celsius.

Exercise

Using the example above, write a program to convert degrees Fahrenheit to degrees Celsius. Then add another #define macro to allow the user to convert degrees Celsius to degrees Fahrenheit.

3.4 The if Statement

The `if` statement is fairly crucial to any advanced programming in C: it enables the computer to compare the value of any variable against a set of parameters. For example, is x less than 10 if x is equal to 5? Yes! Is x greater than 7 if x is equal to 5? No! With this yes and no, we can make our program respond to our questions. The basic structure of an `if` statement runs like this:

```
if([conditions to be fulfilled are true]){
    [then do this];
}
```

If the conditions are true, then the program looks inside the curly braces. Otherwise, the program ignores whatever is inside them and carries on. For example,

```
int cakes_eaten = 4;

if(cakes_eaten == 4){
    printf("You are a pig!");
}
```

would print "You are a pig!" to screen, whereas this program:

```
int cakes_eaten = 3;

if(cakes_eaten == 4){
    printf("You are a pig!");
}
```

would not.

3.4.1 Operators

In order to construct meaningful `if` statements, one must use operators. These help compare values within the program and are the tools for the job. Here's a list:

Symbol	Meaning
<	Less than
>	More than
<=	Less than or equal to
>=	More than or equal to
==	Equal to
&&	AND
||	OR
!=	NOT equal to

Table 3.1: A summary of logical operators in C

3.4.2 AND, OR, NOT

These are known as logical operators. They enable us to build computer chips and circuit boards. Here's how we can use them in our simple example:

The OR Operator

```
int cakes_eaten = 5;

if(cakes_eaten == 4 || cakes_eaten > 5){
    printf("You are a pig!");
}
```

This program says, "if you've eaten 4 cakes OR more than 5 cakes, then you are a pig"!

The AND Operator

```
int cakes_eaten = 5;
int cakes_remaining = 1;

if(cakes_eaten >= 4 && cakes_remaining == 0){
    printf("You are a pig and have left none for anyone else!");
}
```

This program says, "if you've eaten 4 cakes or more AND there are no cakes left, then you are a pig and have left none for anyone else!"

The NOT Operator

The NOT operator makes everything the opposite of what it really is:

```
int cakes_remaining = 1;

if(cakes_remaining != 0){
    printf("You are sensible and have left some cakes for other people.");
}
```

This program says, "if there are cakes remaining, then you are sensible and have left some cakes for other people".

3.4.3   Example if Statement Program

Here's an example program containing if statements:

```
/* * * * * * * * * * * * * * * * * * * * * * * * * * * * * * * * * *
* Title: Cakes
* Author: M. Gentile
* Date: 26th February 2012
* Description: This program asks how many cakes the user has eaten... and
*              then prints an appropriate message!
* * * * * * * * * * * * * * * * * * * * * * * * * * * * * * * * * */

#include <stdio.h>
#include <stdlib.h>

int main(void){

    int food, eaten;

    printf("How many cakes have you got?");
    scanf("%d", &food);
    printf("How many cakes have you eaten?");
    scanf("%d", &eaten);

    if(food==1){ //Or, if there is just one cake, then...
        printf("Can I have it please?");
    }
    else if(food==0){ //Or, if there are no cakes, then...
        printf("Disappointing!");
    }
```

```
    //Or, if there are a negative number OR more than 50 cakes, then...
    else if(food<0 || food>50){
        printf("You're being silly!");
    }
    if(food!=0){ //If there are NOT no cakes, then...
        printf("More to share! Can I have one?");
    }
    //Or, if there are no cakes AND you've eaten more than one, then...
    else if(food==0 && eaten > 1){
        printf("You greedy pig!");
    }

    return 0;
}
```

In fact, we've also used `else` statements in the above program too. All an `else` statement means is "if the if previous `if` statement didn't work, then do this..."

Exercises

For either of these exercises, you will need the random-number generator from Section 2.11.

1. Write a "guess the number" game. You will need to use a few if statements. Start by creating a game with guessing a random number between 1 and 100 and then expand it from there.
2. Write a lottery program, which will generate 6 random numbers only the computer knows. Allow the user to enter their six numbers. Make the computer give a different reward for a different number of exact number matches (this program will need AND and OR statements).

3.5 Switches

In C, a switch is an elegant way of selecting a particular response given by the user to a particular multi-choice question asked by the program. Usually, the response is an integer, but it can also be a single character. The question, "Do you want to quit, (y/n)?" is a good example for when a switch statement would be a good idea. The flowchart below demonstrates how a switch works:

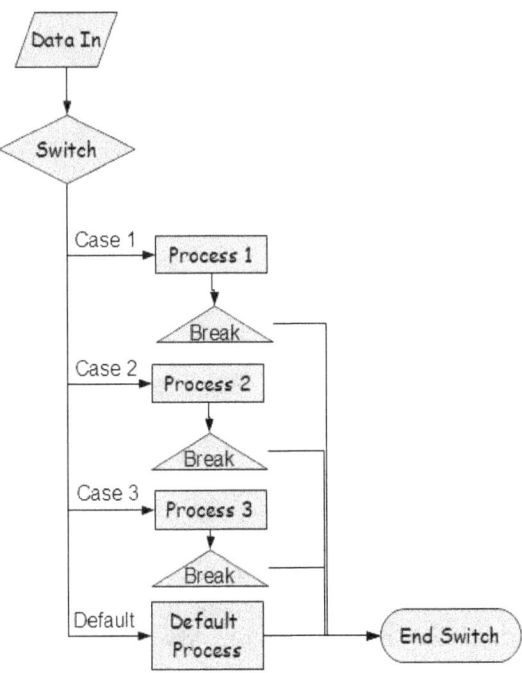

Figure 3.3: A flowchart to show how the switch statement works. Firstly, the data from the user enters the switch. Then the program finds the correct response to give to the answer given. If no responses are correct, then the default process is given, before exiting the switch. Note how the program tries to flow from one process to another, unless there are break statements in-between!

Let's take a programming example. The following program asks us whether we prefer cats or dogs:

```c
/* * * * * * * * * * * * * * * * * * * * * * * * * * * * * * * * * * * * * * * *
 * Title: Cats or Dogs
 * Author: Mr. M. Gentile
 * Date: 29th February 2012
 * Description: Here we ask the user whether they prefer cats or dogs, then print a message.
 * * * * * * * * * * * * * * * * * * * * * * * * * * * * * * * * * * * * * * * */

#include <stdio.h>
#include <stdlib.h>

int main(){

    int a; //Declare an integer for us to examine
    char line[5]; //Declare a string for us to examine

    printf("Hello! Do you prefer:\n"); //Message on screen:
    printf("1. Cats\n 2. Dogs?\n If neither, press any key.");

    fgets(line, sizeof(line), stdin); //Get the input from the keyboard:
    sscanf(line, "%d", &a); //(scanf is a hideous function: use fgets + sscanf instead).

    switch(a){ //Begin our switch.
        case 1: //If the user entered '1' for cats:
```

```
            printf("Miaow! Me too!\n");
            break; //Get out of the switch.
        case 2: //If the user entered '2' for dogs:
            printf("Woof woof!\n");
            break; //Get out of the switch.
        default: //If the user entered anything else:
            printf("You're obviously not a pet person.\n");
    }
    return 0;
}
```

Two important notes for switches:

- Firstly, always include a `default` option, otherwise the program might crash if given an invalid response. In fact for the default case, you could print a message asking for the response you want, then take the program to a point before the switch started to give the user a second chance. Secondly,
- Secondly, always include a `break` statement at the end of each case. These prevent the program from falling through to the next case process **as well as** the process we really wanted. They kick the program out of the switch and onto the next part of the program. Use them always, unless of course, you want more than one case to happen, which can sometimes be very useful.

Note also that we can have as many cases as we want or need. In our case, we've just got two. Let's now adapt our pets example program to be used for characters instead of numbers:

```
#include <stdio.h>
#include <stdlib.h>

int main(){

    char a; //Declare a character for us to examine
    char line[5]; //Declare a string for us to examine

    printf("Hello! Do you prefer:\n"); //Message on screen:
    printf("c. Cats\n d. Dogs?\n If neither, press any key.");

    fgets(line, sizeof(line), stdin); //Get the input from the keyboard:
    sscanf(line, "%c", &a); //(scanf is a hideous function: use fgets + sscanf instead).

    switch(a){ //Begin our switch.
        case 'c': //If the user entered 'c' for cats:
            printf("Miaow! Me too!\n");
            break; //Get out of the switch.
        case 'd': //If the user entered 'd' for dogs:
            printf("Woof woof!\n");
            break; //Get out of the switch.
        default: //If the user entered anything else:
            printf("You're obviously not a pet person.\n");
    }
    return 0;
}
```

Exercise

Write a quiz game, or a chat bot program, where there are several options to choose from listed on the screen. Use switches to enable the user to make a choice in each case.

3.6   Arrays

Wouldn't it be nice, not to have to declare so many variables sometimes? Just look at the code below to see what I mean:

```
int main(void){

    int data1, data2, data3, data4;

    printf("Enter four numbers: ");
    scanf("%d %d %d %d", &data1, &data2, &data3, &data4);
    printf("%d %d",data1*data2,data3*data4);

    return 0;
}
```

Well, this is where arrays come in! An array is simply a group of variables, all under one banner. Arrays save computer memory and user typing. Also, look at the example program for loading from file (2.10.3); we can only load one team and its score at the moment. But with arrays, that can be changed!

3.6.1   1D Arrays

We've actually already seen these before: under the guise of strings! Remember from Section2.2 that a string is really an array of characters? In the following example, our variable called 'name' is really an array of 5 character variables:

```
char name[5];
```

This is why we **can't** say `name='Anna'` but we **can** say:

```
name[0]='A';
name[1]='n';
name[2]='n';
name[3]='a';
name[4]='\0';
```

These parts of the string (or array elements) are just characters. The final array element in a string must be equal to `\0` to indicate the end of the string.

In order to declare arrays of numbers, we do a similar process:

```
int data[4];
```

This creates **five** integer variables to play with: `data[0]`, `data[1]`, `data[2]`, `data[3]` and `data[4]`.

An Example Where Arrays Are Useful

The program below asks for the ages of five different people and then prints them all out again. This entire program is only 8 lines long, compared to twice that if arrays were not used.

```
/* * * * * * * * * * * * * * * * * * * * * * * * * * * * * * * * * *
 * Title: Ages
 * Author: M. Gentile
 * Date: 26th February 2012
 * Description: This program asks the ages of five different people, stores
 *              them in an array and then prints them out again.
 * * * * * * * * * * * * * * * * * * * * * * * * * * * * * * * * * */

#include <stdio.h>
#include <stdlib.h>
```

```
int main(void){

    int i; //Create a counting integer
    int age[4]; //Create an array of 5 integers

    for(i=0; i<5; i++){ //Ask the age of each person in turn.
        printf("How old is person %d?",i);
        scanf("%d", &age[i]);
    }
    for(i=0; i<5; i++){ //Print the age of each person out in turn.
        printf("Person %d is %d years old.\n", i, age[i]);
    }

    return 0;
}
```

Exercise:

Change the football loading program in section 2.10.3 so that the points and the team name for ten different teams are stored in two arrays. Then alter the program to make it load every team name and score, not just one as in the example. You'll need to use a `for` loop here's a tip: `fgets` goes onto the next line of the file every time it is used, so using it twice would read in the first two lines of the file in question. Also, you will need to create a text file to be read by the program in this format:

```
Manchester_City 63
Manchester_United 61
Tottenham_Hotspur 53
Arsenal 46
Chelsea 46
Newcastle_United 43
```

etc. (this is the `%s %d` format). If it is in this format, you'll need to use `sscanf` in the format `"%s %d"` to read in the team name, then the score respectively.

3.6.2 2D Arrays

Sometimes, it's even useful to create an array of arrays! For example, if I want a program to handle a database of students' test scores, then I could define an array like so:

```
int scores[STUDENTS][TEST];
```

where the previously defined number STUDENTS is the number of students and TEST is the number of tests which have been carried out. Remember, this 2D array is a variable which stores a single student's score. There is then an array of them, an array of scores, one for each test. Then there is an array of **them** , one for each student. Therefore, an entire database is built, just with one declaration! If there are 30 students and 5 tests, then that's 150 scores, all in one 2D array! Let's see an example of how we can use it:

```
#define STUDENTS 30
#define TEST 5

int main(void){

    int scores[STUDENTS][TEST];
    int test_no, i;

    [Then some code to read in the scores from file]

    printf("Which test scores would you like to look at?\n");
```

```
    scanf("%d", &test_no);
    printf("Test scores from test %d:\n", test_no);
    printf("Student ID Score");
    printf("---------- -----");
    for(i=0; i<STUDENTS; i++){
        printf("%d  %d", i, scores[i][test_no]);
    }

    return 0;
}
```

So this program prints out all of the results from all of the students under one particular test, entered in by the user.

Exercise

Adapt your football league table program from the previous exercise to include other leagues. For this, you will need to create other files with teams and points from other leagues. You will also need to have a 2D array storing the points of each team like this: `int points[league][team]` where `league` and `team` are numbers.

3.7 Structures

Structures are a useful way of organising lots of variables into one block. This is useful, because we can effectively create our own objects by this method. Structures are made up from the information contained in our object. For example, in a card game program such as hearts, or solitaire, we can create a structure to make a card. The information required in order to make a card is:

- The card's value
- The suit
- It's colour
- Whether it's in play or not

3.7.1 Defining & Creating Structures

So let's create a playing card template! Remember, we're going to create our own object here, so what we're going to do in effect is define an entirely new type of variable: not an int or a char this time, but a card.

```
typedef struct card { //Declare our structure and give it a name (now called struct card).

    int value; //The value of the card from 2 to 14 (for Ace)
    char suit; //The suit of the card (either H, D, S or C).
    char colour[3]; //The colour of the card (either Red or Blk)
    int involved; //Whether the card is involved in play or not (0 for no, 1 for yes)

} Card; //Give our structure a better name: 'Card'.
```

From now on, whenever we declare a variable Card, it can now hold the 4 pieces of information as defined above.

In order to go ahead and create cards within our program, the first step is to declare a new Card structure and give it a name, like so:

```
Card one_card;
Card many_cards[52];
```

The Card type variable named one_card is just one card. The Card type variable many_cards is an array (52 in fact) of cards. A deck in fact! It's always possible to create an array of structures.

3.7.2 Adding Information to Structures

The next step is to add information to the structures. It's best to show an example for the Ace of Hearts:

```
one_card.value = 14;
one_card.suit = 'H';
strcpy(one_card.colour,"Red"); //Make sure you include <string.h> for this one.
one_card.involved = 0;
```

You see, we access each variable within our Card structure by put a dot after the structure's name, then the variable name. After that, we're free to set the value to whatever we like! Similarly, the same is true of the array of cards, again for the Ace of Hearts:

```
many_cards[0].value = 14;
many_cards[0].suit = 'H';
strcpy(many_cards[0].colour,"Red"); //Make sure you include <string.h> for this one.
many_cards[0].involved = 0;
```

3.7.3 Cylinder Volume Program

This program uses structures to help calculate the volume of a cylinder.

```c
/****************************************************************/
/*Title: Cylinder Volume Finder */
/*Author: M. Gentile */
/*Date: 26-2-12 */
/*Description: This program computes the volume of a cylinder. */
/****************************************************************/

#include <stdio.h>
#include <stdlib.h>

typedef struct cylinder{ //Define what we mean by a 'cylinder'
    float height; //How tall the cylinder is
    float radius; //How wide the cylinder is
} Cylinder; //Call it a sensible name, 'Cylinder'

int print_volume(Cylinder a); //Prototype our function for later

int main(void){
    Cylinder tube; //Declare a cylinder type structure and call it 'tube'.

    printf("Enter the radius of your cylinder.\n");
    scanf("%f",&tube.radius); //Scan for radius.
    printf("Enter the height of your cylinder.\n");
    scanf("%f",&tube.height); //Scan for height.

    print_volume(tube); //Compute the volume

    return 0;
}

//This function takes in a cylinder structure and computes its volume.
int print_volume(Cylinder a){ //a is 'any old cylinder'.

    #define PI 3.14159265 //Define pi.

    float volume; //Declare a float for the volume.

    volume = PI * a.radius * a.radius * a.height; //Use formula to compute the volume.
    printf("The volume of your cylinder is %f", volume); //Print result to screen.

    return 0;
}
```

Exercise

Write an address book program which stores a person's name, address and telephone number. You will need to create a structure which stores this information and call it a sensible name (say, Person for example). You will then need to create an array of persons e.g. Person people[10] would create 10 entries. Once the data is added, save it to file, so that it can be viewed again on request. For instance, if I want to list all the names entered, then I would print each people[i].name string in a for loop (where i is an integer). N.B. You will need to use fgets to read in the addresses, not scanf!

3.8 Pointers

Pointers are very useful to be able to grasp properly: they save declaring lots of variables, freeing up memory and therefore making your program work faster. We have already come across pointers, under the guise of saving and loading to files.

3.8.1 What Pointers Are

Pointers are not real things in themselves: pointers are merely signposts to real things, like files for example. Or structures. In fact, pointers can point to anything, whether it be an integer, float, character, string, file or structures. Then when we tell the pointer to change its value, the real thing changes its value too.

3.8.2 Declaring Pointers

Pointers can be declared under any variable type. For an example, let's declare two floats and two float-type pointers:

```
float john, simon, *p, *q; // p and q are pointers, john and simon are actual floats.
```

We always put a * infront of the pointer when declaring a pointer.

3.8.3 Pointing Pointers at Things

As a next step, we need to point our pointers at things. This is a crucial step: non-referenced pointers are entirely useless. In order to show how to point a pointer at a variable, let's take an example of pointing our two pointers (above) at our two float variables:

```
p = &john;
q = &simon;
```

The & means, "Where this variable is". This is called the **address** of the variable. So, pointer p has now written down the address of john for future reference. We can look at this address by using the identifier for a pointer, which is %p:

```
printf("Address of john and value of p: %p \n");
printf("Value of john and *p: %f \n", p, *p);
```

At the moment, the value of john is 0.00, so the value of *p is also 0.00, because p points towards john, giving this value. Therefore, if change the value of *p, we change the value of john too. For instance:

```
*p = 1.5;
*q = 8.9;
```

Would change the value of john from 0.00 to 1.5 and the value of simon to 8.9.

3.8.4 Pointers and Structures

It is much easier to use pointers coupled with structures than to deal with structures directly. Let's recall our cylinder example structure program:

```
typedef struct cylinder{ //Define what we mean by a 'cylinder'

    float height; //How tall the cylinder is
    float radius; //How wide the cylinder is

} Cylinder; //Call it a sensible name, 'Cylinder'
```

In our main program, we can now declare a Cylinder and a pointer to point to the cylinder, thus:

```
int main(void){

    Cylinder tube; //Real cylinder
    Cylinder *t;  // Point to the cylinder

    (*t).height = 10.0; //This would work, but it's much easier to do:
    t->height = 10.0; // = Much less typing!
```

3.8.5   Passing Pointers to Functions

We can even call functions using pointers. This is very fluid and can help make the program flow more quickly. I've adapted the cylinder example program to show how this is done:

```
/***************************************************************/
/*Title: Cylinder Volume Finder */
/*Author: M. Gentile */
/*Date: 26-2-12 */
/*Description: This program computes the volume of a cylinder, */
/*             but this time uses pointers.                     */
/***************************************************************/

#include <stdio.h>
#include <stdlib.h>

typedef struct cylinder{ //Define what we mean by a 'cylinder'

    float height; //How tall the cylinder is
    float radius; //How wide the cylinder is
    float volume; //The volume of the cylinder

} Cylinder; //Call it a sensible name, 'Cylinder'

int print_volume(Cylinder *t); //Prototype our function for later

int main(void){

    Cylinder tube; //Declare a cylinder type structure and call it 'tube'.

    printf("Enter the radius of your cylinder.\n");
    scanf("%f",&tube.radius); //Scan for radius.
    printf("Enter the height of your cylinder.\n");
    scanf("%f",&tube.height); //Scan for height.

    print_volume(&tube); //Compute the volume

    return 0;
}

//This function takes in a cylinder structure and computes its volume.
int print_volume(Cylinder *t){ //a is 'any old cylinder'.

    #define PI 3.14159265

    //Use the formula to compute the volume.
    t->volume = PI * t->radius * t->radius * t->height;

    //Print the result to screen.
```

```
    printf("The volume of your cylinder is %f", t->volume);

    return 0;
}
```

Essentially, all that is changed it the structure and the function. The main program remains largely the same, except this time I'm feeding the **address** of the Cylinder to the function, not the entire Cylinder structure. Also, I haven't got to declare any new variables inside the function: the function changes the **actual value** of the volume contained within the Cylinder structure fed to it. This is powerful stuff! It uses much less memory, it keeps our variables neat and tidy and it saves on typing. Win-win!

Exercise

Change your address book program so that it uses pointers to change the entries in the address book. You will need a string pointer for the names and addresses and an integer pointer for the phone numbers.

Chapter 4

Advanced Programming in C

These sections in detail are beyond the scope of this book. But I introduce them here for you the reader to go away and research them for yourself if you find the concepts either interesting or useful.

4.1 Memory Allocation

It is much better to use less RAM than more. By efficiently allocating memory, we can make our programs run more swiftly. This matters if we are creating programs on slower systems, or creating large numbers of variables which require lots of memory to handle. The main function we use to allocate RAM is `malloc`. If we require more memory, then we use `realloc`. When we've stopped using the memory, then we free the RAM again by using the `free` function. An example use for this is dynamic allocation of variable lengths. If we don't know how long a variable is going to be before it is entered, then we can allocate an amount of memory to it as needs must. This then saves the system's memory resources.

4.2 Linked Lists

Linked lists are essentially a lot of structures all linked to each other by pointers. One pointer in each structure points to address of the next structure, in order to tie the two together. This is particularly useful in programming things such as card games: when dealing the deck of cards, the next card will follow on from the previous one quite fluidly. Of course, when shuffling the deck, every pointer must be re-assigned in one continuous and non-repeating loop.

4.3 Binary Trees

Binary trees are a way of rapidly storing and retrieving data: essentially, all the data stored in the tree is sorted from left to right, with the data with the least value stored on one side of the tree and the data with the most value stored on the other.

4.4 Recursion

The whole concept of recursion is essentially a function which calls itself if it hasn't finished its job. This is useful in some circumstances.

Index